Dear Carolyn and Michael,

Though I'm feeling just fine, my affairs in order (as they say) very important, you need to k riting this.

After looking through the large manila envelope addre m sure you'll eventually come

Clint Eastwood

Meryl Streep

THE

BRIDGES OF

WARNER BOOKS

A Time Warner Company

MADISON

COUNTY

THE FILM

Photographs by Ken Regan

Warner Books, Inc.,
1271 Avenue of the Americas,
New York, NY 10020

A Time Warner Company

Printed in the United States of America
First Printing: June 1995
10 9 8 7 6 5 4 3 2 1
ISBN: 0-446-51997-9 LC: 95-60626

Based on the Novel by Robert James Waller

Design by Walter Bernard and Milton Glaser

Design Assistants: Chalkley Calderwood, Nancy Eising. Picture Editor: Suzanne Regan

Francesca Johnson's children, Carolyn and Michael, arrive at their old family's farm in Madison County, Iowa, after the death of their mother. A family lawyer is present to tie up unfinished business—and to inform the children of a surprising request made by Francesca in her last will and testament.

❧ In a recent addition to her will, the lawyer announces, Francesca Johnson has asked not to be buried next to her husband in the family graveyard plot, but to be cremated and have her ashes scattered from the Roseman covered bridge.

Confused by the request, Michael assures everyone that it must be a mistake and adamantly refuses to throw his mother's ashes to the wind. She will be buried beside their father.

As the others sort through legal papers, Carolyn finds an envelope postmarked 1965. Enclosed is a photograph of her mother, looking somehow both radiant and sad, at the Roseman Bridge. She also finds a small key.

The key opens a trunk at the foot of their mother's bed. Inside, Michael and Carolyn find journals and a letter addressed to them from their mother: *"How sad it seems to me to leave this earth without those you love the most ever really knowing who you were. . . . His name was Robert Kincaid."*

Francesca begins her story in the summer of 1965 as her husband and children were setting off to show a prized steer at the state fair. It seemed terrible, she knew, but Francesca really couldn't wait for her husband and children to leave. It had been so long since she had had even a moment to herself; to have four whole days and nights seemed an unimaginable luxury.

Day One

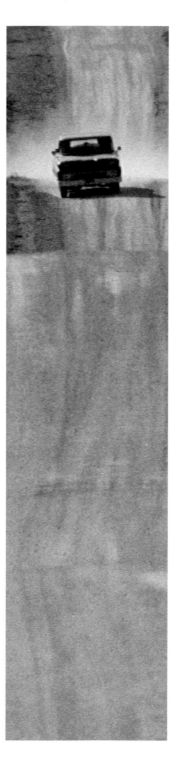

🐦 *National Geographic* photographer Robert Kincaid drove into Madison County, Iowa, to shoot its famed covered bridges.

ɋ Francesca watched the truck pull into the driveway.

Robert wanted directions for the Roseman Bridge.

🍂 At first, Francesca was wary of the long-haired out-of-towner.

Then, on an impulse, she offered to show him the way.

  The whole of Robert's life seemed to be crammed into every corner of the truck. Sitting in this private world of a man she hardly knew, the act of lighting a cigarette became a gesture of intimacy . . . and excitement.

Francesca felt peculiarly liberated–free, for a while, from all she knew and all who knew her.

She was a little embarrassed by her own spying, but she liked watching the way his body moved as he worked, efficiently, like someone who had made the same motions so many times that they had become part of him.

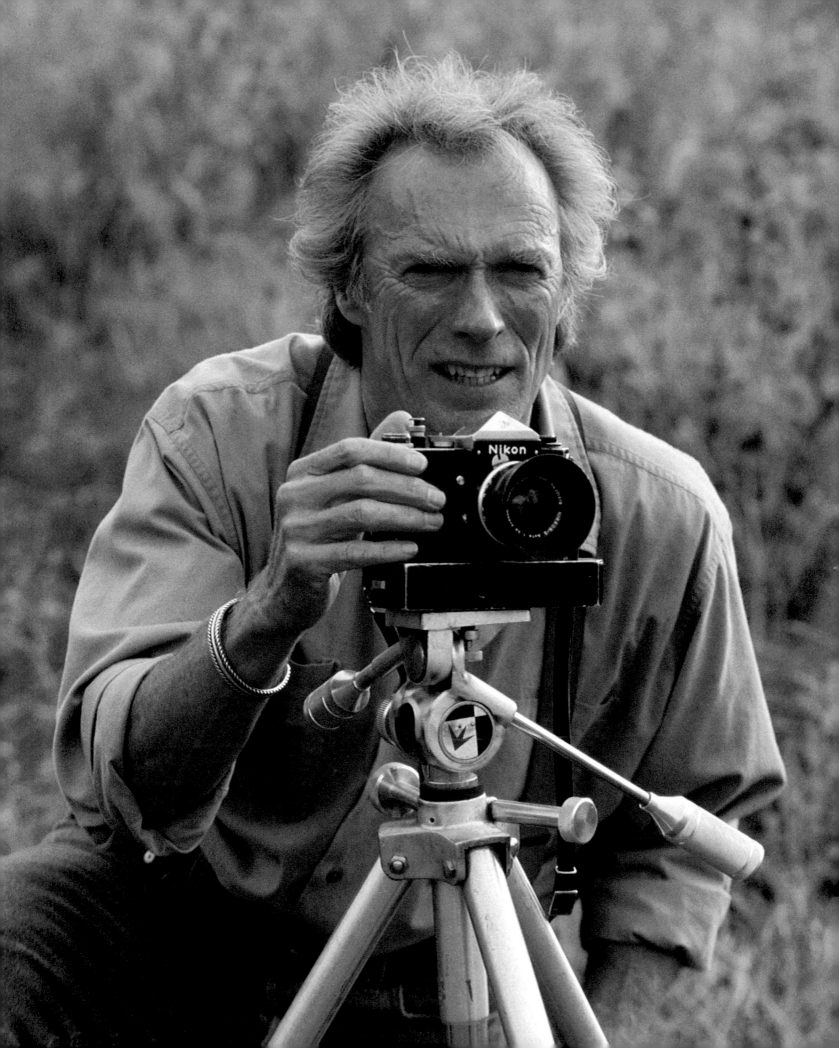

🌺 "Men still give women flowers, don't they?" Robert asks, with thanks for her help.

Francesca nods: "Except those are poisonous."

Back at the house, drinking iced tea, she tells him a little about Italy, Iowa, her life.

She realizes she doesn't want him to go and asks, "Would you like to stay for dinner?"

🌸 Francesca caught herself pausing by the window, gazing at Robert as he washed up for dinner.

Robert surprises Francesca with an offer to help her prepare dinner.

The stories he tells—of making pictures of gorillas in Africa, of spontaneously getting off a train in Italy— delight and enthrall Francesca. She asks to hear more of his adventures— unless he's too tired. "You're asking a man if he's too tired to talk about himself? You don't get out much, do you?" he teases.

She had been saving the brandy for an occasion, but one hadn't come along. This, she decides, is it. "To ancient evenings and distant music," toasts Robert.

Francesca suffers a brief moment of panic about the evening's activities. "We're not doing anything wrong, you know," says her guest, as if he has read her mind. She relaxes.

As brother and sister finish reading part of their mother's journal, Michael is becoming increasingly indignant. "He's getting her drunk," he says. The two argue about Robert Kincaid's character. Michael maintains that he's a would-be adulterer and all-around bad guy; Carolyn that he's no worse than her own husband. Michael is distressed to find that all is not well with his sister. She picks up the diary again . . .

As Robert pulls out of her driveway, the telephone rings. It is Richard, at the state fair.

Distracted, Francesca can barely focus on the conversation. She hangs up with relief.

As she looks in the mirror, it occurs to Francesca that it has been a long time since she has looked at herself as a woman.

She writes a note: "If you'd like supper again '*when white moths are on the wing,*' come by tonight after you're finished. Anytime is fine." She will leave it at the bridge for him.

Day Two

❦ It is dawn. The sound of an old pickup truck awakens Francesca, and for a moment she sits up in bed. As she settles back to sleep, Robert arrives at the Roseman Bridge. At first, he does not see the note tacked to the structure.

The photographer has only a brief period when the morning light is just right for his pictures. Robert pockets the note without reading it so he can finish shooting. Meanwhile, Francesca waits for a response.

☙ As she is putting the tractor back in the barn, Francesca thinks she hears the phone ringing. She dashes for the house.

"Hi. This is Robert Kincaid. Got your note."

They arrange to meet at Holliwell Bridge.

Over a cup of coffee in Winterset, Robert gets an earful of small-town gossip.

Francesca heads out for Des Moines, where she buys groceries, wine and then—guiltily—a new dress.

When Robert gets another dose of gossip about a local woman in the general store, he realizes that Francesca may be risking her reputation to see him. He calls her back.

"If it's a problem for you to see me tonight, given the curiosity of small-town people, don't feel pressured," he says. She hesitates: "I'll meet you at the bridge just like we planned."

She enjoys watching him work, but is embarrassed to be caught by the camera.

  After a hot evening of shooting, Francesca and Robert return to clean up for dinner. Lying in the bath after Robert has showered, Francesca has to acknowledge the depth of her attraction: "Lying where the water had run down his body was intensely erotic."

  ❧ Wearing the new dress, she meets him in the kitchen. She takes a call from a chatty neighbor. She touches him. "If you don't mind my boldness, you look stunning," he says.

The radio plays a blues song. Robert takes Francesca in his arms, and they dance. She is shaking. Finally, he whispers, "If you want me to stop, tell me now."

74

Day Three

🕊 After a night of making love they decide to spend the day away from Madison County.

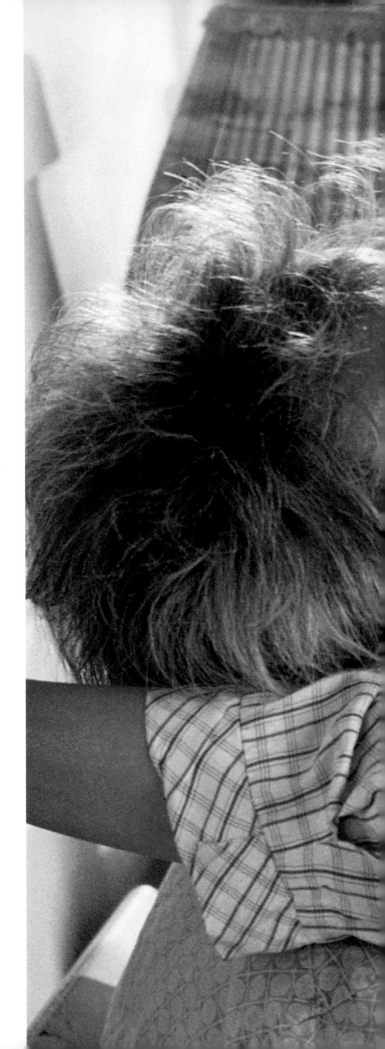

After a picnic, they wind up at a roadhouse where they begin to realize just how short their time is. Richard and the children will soon be home. They have one more day.

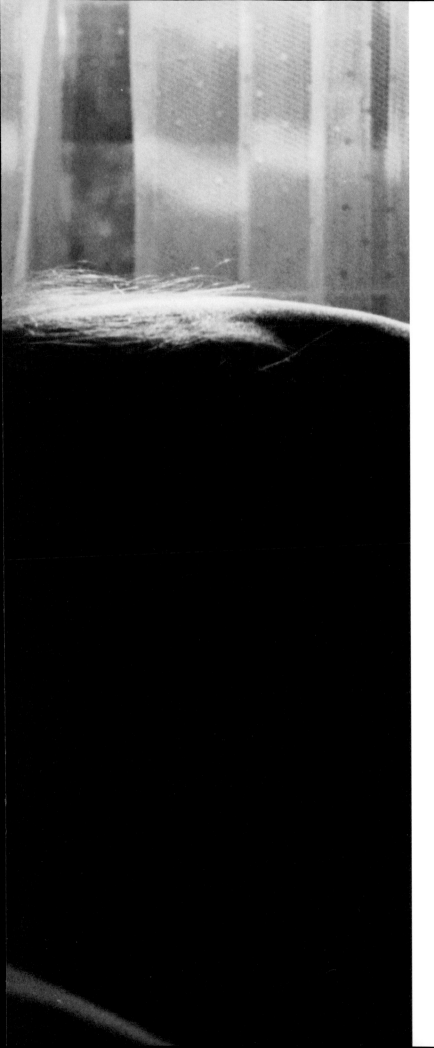

That evening, they made love with the tenderness and familiarity of two people who had known one another all their lives—but what of their future? "I was up all that night," Francesca wrote. "What happens tomorrow?"

After reading about their mother's affair, Michael and Carolyn need to get out of the house and talk. They share a bottle of whiskey and confidences.

Day Four

☙ With the morning comes an uneasiness and uncertainty. Francesca needs to know: Is this just another affair or does he love her the way she loves him? "I don't want to need you," he cries. "Why?" she asks. "Because I can't have you."

❧ "I've got to know the truth, Robert, or I'll go crazy," Francesca pleads. "I can't pretend I don't feel what I feel because it's over tomorrow."

Finally Robert admits . . . "Right now, it looks like the only thing I've done all my life was to make my way to you," he says. "If I even think about leaving—" They hear a car. It's an ill-timed neighborly visit.

She tries to listen to Madge as she chatters, but all she can think of is Robert waiting for her upstairs. Robert, the man who loves her and is going to ask her to leave everything she knows.

"Come with me," he says as she lies down on the bed next to him. But as she packs her suitcases, she is pulled by the familiar scenes of her home.

❧ Seeing her face, he knows. "You're not coming with me, are you?" She tells him,
"I want to love you the way I do now for the rest of my life."

❧ "I can't say good-bye yet," he says. As she runs to him one last time, she tears a button from her dress. It falls by the gate. Robert tells her he will be in town a few more days. If they see each other again, maybe she will change her mind.

The return of responsibilities brings Francesca a feeling of safety, of thankfulness for what she has. Each time she thinks of Robert, a detail of everyday life intrudes, binding her to the reality she has always known.

🐚 Then, while shopping in
town, Francesca sees Robert.
Without a word exchanged,
Robert knows what Francesca's
tears mean. And he decides in
that moment to give her up.

KINCAID PE

🍂 At supper, Richard gives her the button he has found by the front gate. "... *I almost told him ...*" she wrote to her children. "... *If he really loved me, maybe he'd understand.*" That night Francesca pays a visit to "that Redfield woman," the one person in all of Winterset with whom she could think of Robert and their love without shame.

As the sun rises, Michael and Carolyn are finishing their mother's journal.
"... *I received Robert's letter soon after. I always wondered if your father found it ...*"

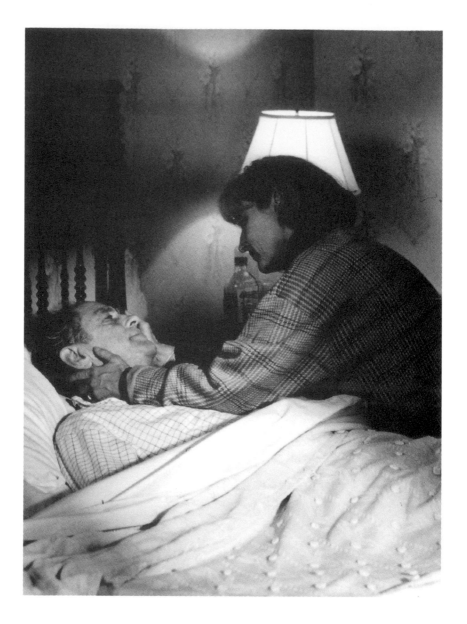

🌢 Before he died, Richard told her: "I know you had your own dreams. I am sorry I couldn't give them to you." Later, she tried to find Robert, but couldn't. Every year, she revisited the spots they had been together. Then she received a letter from his lawyer, informing her that Robert had passed away, leaving her his effects. *"There has not been a day since, that I have not thought of him . . ."*

". . . If it hadn't been for him, I don't think I would have lasted on the farm . . ." Carolyn found the dress her mother had bought for her special dinner. And she and Michael agreed they must throw their mother's ashes from the Roseman Bridge.

Principal Cast

ROBERT KINCAID...Clint Eastwood

FRANCESCA JOHNSON ....Meryl Streep

RICHARD JOHNSON.. Jim Haynie

CAROLINE JOHNSON... Annie Corley

MICHAEL JOHNSON..Victor Slezak

YOUNG CAROLINE...Sarah Schmidt

YOUNG MICHAEL...Chris Kroon

BETTY...Phyllis Lyons

MADGE...Debra Monk

LAWYER ....Richard Lage

LUCY REDFIELD...Michelle Benes

WARNER BROS. Presents

An AMBLIN/MALPASO Production CLINT EASTWOOD MERYL STREEP "THE BRIDGES OF MADISON COUNTY" Music by LENNIE NIEHAUS
Screenplay by RICHARD LaGRAVENESE Based on the novel by ROBERT JAMES WALLER Produced by CLINT EASTWOOD and KATHLEEN KENNEDY
Directed by CLINT EASTWOOD

Soundtrack on Malpaso Cassettes & CDs

THE CAST AND CREW OF *THE BRIDGES OF MADISON COUNTY* GATHER AT THE FARMHOUSE IN IOWA.

A Visit to Madison County

*"I ask myself over and over,
'What happened to me
in Madison County, Iowa?'"*
—ROBERT KINCAID,
The Bridges of Madison County (the novel)

*"I'm here to make a film about
a man and a woman
who fall in love completely."*
—CLINT EASTWOOD,
The Bridges of Madison County (the film),
Winterset, Iowa, September 1994

DIRECTOR EASTWOOD
EYEBALLS A LONG SHOT
THROUGH THE CORNSTALKS
NEAR ROSEMAN BRIDGE.

THERE REALLY IS A MADISON COUNTY IN IOWA, AND IT REALLY DOES have covered bridges. These are facts you can hang onto in this tangled-up skein of reality and fantasy. The yarn begins with the real bridges in the real Madison County, where just a few years ago the 12,483 real residents of the county were minding their own business—with no idea that their home in the heart of the heartlands, just a half hour southwest of Des Moines, was about to become the romantic county seat of the world.

One day, the story goes, Robert James Waller, a 50-year-old economics professor on sabbatical from the University of Northern Iowa, was driving his pickup truck through the rolling corn and soybean fields of Madison County, his camera bag by his side. He had been taking pictures of the local covered bridges, and he was humming a bossa nova tune he had written about a woman named Francesca. He says that at that moment the whole saga of Francesca Johnson and Robert Kincaid popped into his head. He went home to Cedar Falls, Iowa, and wrote his novel in just two weeks. That was in July 1990. He found an agent and then a publisher, Maureen Egen at Warner Books. In April 1992, 18,000 copies of Waller's 171-page book quietly appeared in stores.

Not long after that, Sherry Ellis was sitting in her office at the Madison County Chamber of Commerce in the county seat of Winterset (pop. 4,198). After working as a sheriff's dispatcher and jail keeper, she had just taken a post as the Chamber's executive vice president. She handled requests for perhaps 10 tourist packets a week. But on that day, a month after she took the job, everything changed.

"A young lady from California walked in the door carrying a small hardback book," recalls Ellis.

Said the out-of-towner, "I don't know how you can stand to live in such a romantic place."

Ellis was a little confused. Romantic? Winterset? she asked herself. Yes, John Wayne's birthplace was here. Yes, they had the Covered Bridge Festival every fall. The Delicious apple was discovered here, and the County Courthouse, built in 1876, was a historic landmark. But romantic?

That July afternoon, Ellis drove the 35 miles to Des Moines to buy the little book. She finally located it in the "Of Iowa Interest" section. "A box of tissues later," she called the book's author and invited him to the Covered Bridge Festival that fall. They ordered 500 books for him to autograph, figuring that would be plenty. After two hours, they ran out and had to scour Des Moines for every available copy. The next day, Waller signed another 1,000 books. Madison County was on the map.

Back in Hollywood, Kathleen Kennedy had already heard of Madison County. An astute producer who had worked with Steven Spielberg as president of his Amblin Productions since 1984, she had made many of the megahits of movieland—*E.T.*, *Jurassic Park*, *Back to the Future*, *Roger Rabbit*, *Gremlins*—and she was looking for something different. "I've always believed that if you could find a really nice little romance, you could make a nice, quiet little movie," she says. She read *The Bridges of Madison County* in manuscript, and it caught her eye. "I liked that it was mature, not about a couple of 20-year-olds," says Kennedy, a trim businesswoman of 41. "I found it moving. It brought to the surface a lot of feelings and issues. For me it tapped into something deeper than a mid-life affair. I believe that a lot of people have the potential to fall in love with any number of people. You don't know what fate has in store." Kennedy had the presence of mind to purchase from the author's agent, Aaron Priest, an option on the movie rights to the novel. She says, "I didn't know it was an enormous phenomenon about to happen."

Indeed, no one could have predicted that by January of 1993 word-of-mouth would have propelled the little book to No. 1 on the *New York Times* bestseller list. By the spring, when newly planted fields were greening, Madison County itself had been featured on television shows by Charles Kuralt and Oprah Winfrey. By the time the corn was knee high, video crews were showing up to shoot *The Madison County Waltz*, a VH1 promotional video for balladeer Robert Waller's debut Atlantic Records album, and news crews from NBC, CBS, ABC and CNN were covering the multimedia phenomenon.

CLINT EASTWOOD AND MERYL STREEP GET INTO THE MOVIEMAKING MOOD AT HOLLIWELL BRIDGE.

W INTER SET IN AGAIN IN WINTERSET. BY JANUARY 1994, THE BOOK had been on the bestseller list, usually at No. 1, for more than a year. Several thousands of the citizens of Madison County signed a petition asking that the movie be shot there rather than in Canada or Pennsylvania—after all, figures demonstrated that the last movie shot in Iowa, *Field of Dreams*, had injected some $5.6 million into the state's economy. At the end of January, Sherry Ellis of the Madison County Chamber of Commerce and Wendol Jarvis of the Iowa Film Commission flew to Los Angeles to deliver their plea. The Amblin people who met with them assured them that Madison County was being considered as a location. And if the movie was to be shot that summer, something would have to be done quickly.

Producer Kennedy's immediate problem, however, was not location, but a script. A couple of respected scriptwriters had given it a shot, but she wasn't satisfied. Only with the right script could she sign the kind of talent she wanted for the "little movie" that was getting bigger all the time.

Enter Richard Lagravenese. At 34, the screenwriter (*The Fisher King, The Little Princess*) had been married for some eight years and had a daughter of four. Born and raised in New York City, he discussed the book with his friends. It was his sister Patty, a woman of 45, Francesca's age and, like the character, married with two children, who "cinched it for me," he says. "She's the reason I did it. She made me see that this book was speaking to people on a lot of levels." He knew he was taking a risk by adapting such a popular book. "We're in a very cynical period. The cool thing now is to have a hard edge and not too much emotion," he says. "But people are starving for it." He wrote a draft in six weeks.

By the time the fields in Madison County were plowed, location manager Kenny Haber and production designer Jeannine Oppewall had traveled to Iowa. For three days they looked for a deserted farmhouse with a dirt road leading to it. Finally they rented a helicopter and flew a grid over Madison County, identifying about 10 possibilities. "Then, as we were running out of fuel, we went over The Place," Oppewall recalls. "Kenny and I looked at each other and said, 'That's it.' It had the correct relationship to the road, it was large enough to shoot in and clearly not occupied. Well, it was occupied, actually—by raccoons, bats, birds, mice and bees."

IN THE DIRECTOR'S CHAIR, EASTWOOD, WITH HIS CREW, WAITS FOR A SHOT TO BE SET UP.

John Reed, of the Madison County Chamber of Commerce film office, met them at the property. They jumped over the fence, waded through chest-high grass and peered through the windows of the large, 1890s structure. Then they got on the phone to track down the owner, who proved to live in Detroit. By the end of June, they had negotiated a deal to redo the ruin.

Oppewall took an apartment and called in the forces: She had a construction coordinator, four motion picture carpenters, four scenic artists with helpers, two art directors who did drawings, a set decorator with four or five people and 10 to 15 extra hands from Des Moines as needed. Crews tore the three porches off the house, saving materials to use in rebuilding. Footings had to be redone. The screen porch was rebuilt two feet bigger than it had been, for ease of shooting. A new roof of red shingles was laid on top of the old, so that the lines would be soft and sagging rather than sharp and new. Windows and doors were replaced, floors redone. The infrastructure had to be put in place too. The pump to the well was repaired—the property had no running water or plumbing—but it went dry, and they had to truck in water. Telephone and electric lines were run underground to the house. The moviemakers then put up fake phone poles and lines through the field.

THE TRUCK FROM "A PERFECT WORLD" HAS ANOTHER STAR TURN, AS CAMERAMAN STEVE CAMPANELLI SHOOTS INTO THE CAB.

ON THE FOURTH OF JULY, THE BOOK WAS STILL SELLING 150,000 copies a week, and Oppewall was driving around, "getting lost in the landscape." She stopped at a thrift store. There her eye went to a tablecloth, and she found her pallet: "It contained all the colors I wanted to use in that farmhouse." For the kitchen, a green and a warm yellow ocher. For the dining room, green and blood red. Blue green in the hallways. A warm pinkish beige with blue trim for the bedroom. Oppewall had sheet linoleum trucked in from L.A. and cut into an old-fashioned linoleum rug design. In West Des Moines, she spent three days sorting through the traditional wallpaper patterns at Capitol Paint and Wallpaper. She found two other sources for wallpaper as well, one company that stocked antique wallpapers and another that reproduced old styles to order. Once up, the papers had to be toned and aged, sealed and glazed.

BETWEEN TAKES, THE 6'4" DIRECTOR GOES AFTER FLIES ON THE CEILING OF THE FARMHOUSE KITCHEN.

A trailer truckload of furniture was shipped from Warner Bros., which has one of the best prop collections of antique furniture in the country. She had several pieces repainted and recovered. Other pieces were collected locally by scouts who shopped "with cameras," taking Polaroids of possibilities in junk shops and antique malls for purchase after approval.

And Madison County itself helped. "No traffic. No hassle. The people are very generous and very helpful," says Oppewall. Keith Dillin, head of transportation for the film company, worked with the Chamber of Commerce in collecting a data base of period automobiles. A garden had to be created near the house, and the agriculture experts at the University of Iowa, Ames, extension office suggested plants to put in last-minute in August. Oppewall passed one field with immature corn and knocked on the farmer's door, asking, "Do you think we could transplant two rows of your corn?" She reports, "The guy almost died laughing."

The beleaguered Chamber of Commerce, realizing that *The Bridges of Madison County* phenomenon was not going to go away, bought a building and

FOR A CLOSEUP OF STREEP LOOKING
OUT OF THE FARMHOUSE WINDOW, THE
DIRECTOR TAKES A CATBIRD SEAT.

moved to a bigger space. That August, 1,800 visitors signed in at the new office, and the 50,000 tourist brochures produced that summer were all gone. A total of 178 group bus tours were coming through—compared with nine two years earlier. If the filmmakers came to town at the same time as the Covered Bridge Festival—oh, my, thought Ellis.

THE HOLDUPS BACK IN HOLLYWOOD, STILL, WERE CASTING AND SCRIPT. "Cast is key," realized Kennedy when she first thought about making the film. Readers had been casting the roles of Robert Kincaid and Francesca Johnson in their heads all along. Isabella Rossellini, Cher, Angelica Houston. Sam Shepard, Harrison Ford, Robert Redford.

But the actor who seemed best to fit the character of Robert Kincaid, the "last cowboy" hero of the book, was Clint Eastwood, one of the most popular actors in film history. To date, he has starred in 37 films and directed 19. Hollywood's most prolific living filmmaker, Eastwood has made 21 films for Warner Bros. since 1981. He has won Oscars for Best Director and Best Picture for a film that received nine nominations, including Best Actor for his own performance (*Unforgiven*, 1993). He has won an Oscar for Outstanding Achievement in Film (The Irving Thalberg Award, 1995). He is an American icon, and he does not disappoint in person. A lean and muscled 6'4" presence who does not seek attention, he is a man without artifice.

A love story like this one would definitely be something new for moviedom's reigning king of macho. He accepted the role.

Neither Kennedy, Spielberg nor Eastwood liked an early version of the script. "Nobody seemed to be able to make up their minds on who should be in the picture and what line the script should take," says Eastwood. The summer, when the picture had to be shot, was already half over. "I finally told Warner's, 'You're just not going to get this movie done this year if we don't do it now,'" says Eastwood. "We're going to have to charge out of the box and come rolling down the hill real fast."

The studio agreed. Eastwood became the director and co-producer of the film as well as the star. His production company, Malpaso, would join Amblin to get the story to the screen.

STREEP HANDLES THE
JOHN DEERE TRACTOR AS
PROFESSIONALLY AS AN
IOWA FARMHAND.

Eastwood began working with Spielberg on revisions to the script by phone in the evenings. Spielberg was in East Hampton, NY, and Eastwood was "about as far away as you can get" in Mount Shasta, CA. Eastwood said he wanted a slightly less idealistic relationship between the two main characters than that in the book. "We tried to make it more dynamic," he says. "It's about two misfits out in mid-America. They meet up. One is married with children, another a professed loner. And what begins as an innocent friendship becomes a love affair." Yet Eastwood insisted that the movie stay close to its origins. "The book is very simple, and I didn't want to veer too much from that," he says. "There's a reason for that book being a hit—a certain simplicity, a certain fantasy. Though I can't intellectually say what the reason was for its success, I wanted to capture it in the screenplay." Melissa Rooker, Malpaso Director of Development, reconciled the various script changes at the office in Burbank.

Eastwood's notion was to make the actual filming of the picture as simple as the book: to shoot the story straight through, so that the actors' relationship could develop as naturally as the characters'. "You got the house, a little bit of Winterset, the bridge, some country roads—and that's it. It's like an old-fashioned movie, just telling a story," he decided. "No special effects, no matte shots or superimpositions—nothing fancy like that. Just concentrating on storytelling and trying to give as much scope to the simplicity of the picture as you can."

And still, there was no one cast as Francesca. Actresses had been fighting for the role for almost a year. Catherine Deneuve, who was on the 1994 jury of the Cannes Film Festival, of which Eastwood was president, had shown interest in the part. Jacqueline Bisset was also considered. Producer Kennedy heard from many would-be Francescas. "For me, it was astounding to have conversations with Sophia Loren, Claudia Cardinale—every icon," she says. "But as Waller wrote the book, Francesca was 44 or 45, with teenagers at home. You could stretch the age with Kincaid, but the actress's age was tight." Of course, many studio marketing types wanted younger

female leads for better box office appeal, but Eastwood, himself 64, was adamant. He wanted, he said, a woman with lines in her face like his. Says Kennedy, "He dug in his heels and insisted on it. And it was so right."

O N AUGUST 27, 1994, EASTWOOD GOT ON A PLANE FOR IOWA WITH screenwriter Lagravenese. Naturally, they discussed the all-important casting of the female lead. Says Lagravenese, "The search for Francesca was similar to the search for Scarlett—everybody had an idea." Susan Sarandon, Jessica Lange and Meryl Streep all were discussed. "This is a middle-aged love story. It's not about hiring a model," says Lagravenese. "Women have to see themselves in the actress and see her glamorized by love." The best argument for Streep, at the end of the day, says Lagravenese, was that "the movie is so much about two people sitting across the table from one another drinking iced tea. Meryl Streep—she fills that space with something."

EASTWOOD SHOWS CINEMA-TOGRAPHER JACK GREEN AND CAMERAMAN STEVE CAMPANELLI THE SHOT HE HAS IN MIND.

On Monday, Eastwood checked out Madison County, the town of Winterset, the covered bridges. There are only six of them now—one was burned down a decade back by a victim of unrequited love who didn't want the initials he'd carved in the bridge's wooden beam to mock his unhappiness for posterity. Eastwood thought that two of the extant bridges, Roseman and Holliwell, were usable. Eastwood looked around the farmhouse and had a 15-minute chat with Jeannine Oppewall, who would finish her preparations a few days after Labor Day. She wouldn't see him again until two days before they were scheduled to roll, when he'd walk through the house, give her "a big hug," and tell the relieved designer, "This is just what I wanted."

The moment had come to choose Francesca. On Wednesday, Eastwood made the call to Meryl Streep.

Streep had reservations about the project. She hadn't planned to work that fall and had not been a great fan of the book. "I was not carried away by the book as a literary experience," says Streep carefully. "I admit I was blind to its power. But there must be some secret hidden within it. It went straight into people's emotional center." She told Eastwood that she would read the script.

The next morning, the *Bridges* script was delivered to her Connecticut home. "It read like a play," she says. "It was perfect, complete. It was playable, with an emotional arc to it."

She called Eastwood immediately. "I love it," she told him.

"Will you do it?" he asked.

"Yes," she said.

"You know, I like to keep the pace up. We're going to do this in seven or eight weeks," he told her. "Be in Iowa in two weeks."

Streep was stunned. Most of the movies she's done required four or five months. And typically she has a lot more time to prepare for a role. But she felt she had a handle on Francesca. Growing up, she had known an Italian war bride who lived in the same New Jersey neighborhood. Like Francesca, the woman had married a GI and moved to the United States to raise a family. She was dark-haired, had distinctive mannerisms and an accent. "I can close my eyes and see her," says Streep. "We spent so much time as kids imitating her."

BACK AT MALPASO, ALL WAS ACTIVITY. A MOVIE HAD TO BE STARTED IN A couple of weeks. Possibly only Eastwood could have pulled off the tight schedule. His production company is like a repertory theater company, except that it uses, not actors, but the same crew members over and over. Many of the men have worked with Eastwood for 25 years. "I pride myself on casting the crew as well as the cast," he says. "To do a directorial job and be in the picture, you have to have a really good crew, people who understand your shorthand."

He signed on Jack Green, the cinematographer he long ago promoted from camera operator, who has worked with him on some 24 films, most recently *A Perfect World*. He promoted Bill Bannerman, an efficient 34-year-old from Halifax, Nova Scotia, to be his first assistant director.

After the script was locked, the first thing Bannerman did was to break it down scene by scene, character by character, and make a schedule. His primary task was logistics: "My job is to make sure that all the pieces of the puzzle are there for Clint on Day One." Bannerman set dates for when each set needed to be complete. He made schedules for the actors so that the studio could draw up contracts. "Clint's objective was to shoot this film in continuity, a story that takes place in four days shot over seven weeks," says Bannerman. "The relationship needs to develop in a certain pattern. I'd be a fool to schedule a love scene in the first week—it would destroy it for the actors."

Weather is as important a variable in moviemaking as it is in farming. The Iowa weather was the wild card, unpredictable, from fast moving storms to constant sun. The script's story is set in late August. Farm shots had to be done with corn still standing, and beans unharvested. The bridge shots had to be done with leaves still on the trees. "By mid-November, believe me, there are no leaves on the trees in Iowa," says Bannerman. "We were coming into the window of losing the greenery." And 35 to 40 pages of the script were exterior, August. On average, one or two pages of a script, which account for one or two minutes in a finished film, are shot each day. The town shots were less important to shoot early, since there were fewer trees. Bannerman scheduled 50 days from Eastwood's start date of September 15. Eastwood, he knew, likes to shoot six-day weeks.

M ERYL STREEP WAS A LITTLE NERVOUS. ON SEPTEMBER 14, THE film company gathered for a kick-off party at Wellman's Pub in Des Moines, not far from the motel where the crew was staying and about a half hour from the farmhouse location. Streep didn't know anyone in the bar. She had brought her three-year-old, Louisa, to the party along with a babysitter, thinking to use the child as an excuse for early departure. After eating hors d'oeuvres for about an hour, Louisa was getting cranky, and Eastwood hadn't shown up. "He finally came in about ten o'clock," recalls Streep. She had met Eastwood once, at a friend's birthday party a couple of years before, but hadn't talked to him about her role at all since accepting the job.

UNABLE TO MAKE IT TO THE GREEN, THE AVID GOLFER PRACTICES HIS SWING IN DOWN-TOWN WINTERSET.

She and Eastwood sat quietly in a booth, meeting face to face for the first time since engaged on the project. "I was mostly worried that he'd flip out at my appearance," she says. Without forewarning him, she had reverted back to her original hair color, light brown. "I think he was a little shocked. He'd rewritten the story for a blonde—from northern Italy or something. He didn't say anything. He was nonplussed."

Streep said very little herself. She had to go home and rest so that she could get up and work the next morning. "He did say one thing that completely unnerved me," she recalls. "He said, 'I hope you're not going to do a big accent thing.'"

Meryl Streep, famous for her accents—nine times nominated, one of her two Oscars was awarded for her performance as a Polish immigrant in *Sophie's Choice*—did not want to do an accent. "I was afraid to do an accent ever again in my life—they jump on me so for it," she says. But the way she understood the character, Francesca had lived in Italy until she was 20 years old—half her life. "There was no way she wasn't going to have an accent," says Streep. "It was organic to how I saw the character."

SOUND MAN MARVIN LEWIS DISCUSSES AN UPCOMING SCENE WITH THE BOSS.

She didn't sleep well: "That first day is always horrible, and this was doubly horrible," she says. "The next day, I was going to have to open my mouth and speak for the first time."

Shooting began at the beginning, with Kincaid's truck driving into Madison County. In Eastwood tradition, even the pickup was a troupe member: It was the same 1961 GMC used in *A Perfect World*, repainted green, aged with lacquer and with lettering reading, Kincaid Photography, Bellingham, Wash.

In the early scenes Francesca stands on the front porch, beating rugs and watching the truck come toward the house. As Streep put it, Francesca's first impression of Kincaid was, "Who is this person who seems so full of himself? What's he doing in my driveway?"

Slowly, as scripted, Streep and Eastwood began the relationship that is the heart of the movie. Says Eastwood, "We don't play the sexual attraction early." First came friendship. "Pretty much, we went in order," says Streep. "That is so rare. I'd been longing to do a play for a long time, and in a way, this was a like experience." Clint was impressed with Meryl Streep's skills as an actress. Eastwood says, "She just transforms herself—her gestures, her accent, everything."

IN A STOREFRONT, ONE WESTERN
LEGEND MEETS ANOTHER AS EAST-
WOOD POSES WITH A CUTOUT OF
WINTERSET BOY JOHN WAYNE.

P HOTOGRAPHER KEN REGAN, WHO HAD DONE STILLS FOR DIRECTOR Jonathan Demme in *Silence of the Lambs* and *Philadelphia*, was staggered by his first day. Eastwood never said, "Action," but would begin a scene and say, "Let's start." After what Regan thought was a rehearsal, Eastwood said, "That's it" and moved on. Regan went to assistant director Bannerman and explained that, with the movie cameras and bodies between him and the action, he often had just a little crack to shoot through. In the end, he decided, "I couldn't take a chance at missing a shot." He hung six cameras around himself, including two in large housings called Blimps—a special case that makes the click of a camera shutter virtually inaudible, a necessity on a movie set. Says Regan, "I looked like a walking ad for Nikon."

Eastwood invited Streep to look at dailies, the rough film shot each day, and she never missed a session. "I like to see them," says Streep. "It's a little reward at the end of the day." Kennedy, too, watched the first dailies with fascination. She asked Eastwood if he felt he was stretching his skills as an actor for the role. "No," he told her, "for the first time in my life, I feel like I'm just portraying myself." Says Eastwood, "I like Robert Kincaid because he is his own person. He's independent and creative, but he goes about his life quietly. He enjoys who he is and what he does without being irresponsible. He has integrity."

Eastwood was unfazed by the task of making himself a believable photographer. "I've taken a lot of shots," he says. "I'm not a pro, not fast and furious. Ken Regan was good enough to show me the ropes." Regan had talked with Eastwood about giving him lessons in how to move like a photojournalist, but each time they were supposed to meet, some scheduling problem interfered. Finally, Regan went to Iowa, arriving three or four days before production was to begin with some 26 cases of camera equipment. Regan immediately saw that he wouldn't be able to fit all of his gear into a motel room. He rented an apartment, moved in and went out to the nearest 24-hour grocery store to lay in supplies. As he came around one aisle, he bumped into Eastwood, also wheeling a shopping cart. Eastwood told him to come over to the house he'd rented in the morning.

Regan showed up. There were no hangers-on around. "He doesn't have a maid, a driver—he does everything himself," says Regan. Eastwood cooked them up some breakfast, and Regan started in with his lessons. "You're using a camera that's 30 years out of date," explained Regan. "It's like driving an old pickup truck." The old Nikons, in fact, were Regan's own, the ones he himself had used in the '60s during demonstrations, riots, the Vietnam war. He began by showing Eastwood how to load the cameras. How to change a lens, the F-stop, the shutter speed. How to wear a light meter, drape the camera straps—he telescoped the lesson into less than two days. The most important thing, Regan told his pupil, was to move like a professional: "Like a ballet dancer, with grace, assuredness, confidence." He told Eastwood, "Either you look like a professional onscreen, or I'm history—every photographer friend of mine is going to call me up and say I blew it."

Eastwood was reassuring: "Listen, you're going to be on the set every day, and if I'm doing something wrong, you can just tell me."

Asked Regan, "Does that mean I can say, 'Cut!'"

"Not exactly," said Eastwood.

At Holliwell Bridge, Eastwood did his first on-camera photo shoot. In the scene, he smoothly set up his tripod and changed lenses on his Nikon F, circa 1964. Regan made sure that the lenses used were appropriate—they were his, after all. He had already talked to the costume people about making Eastwood's clothing look like that of a man who worked out-of-doors for a living. "The jeans were pressed," says Regan. "The vest pristine, the boots brand new. They had to age them down quite a bit. No photographer in the field dresses like that." Eastwood took the clothes home each night to give them a lived-in look. Regan also made sure that every time Eastwood picked up the camera, it had a fresh roll of film in it, so that the actor would really be taking pictures. Eastwood would shoot about 18 rolls. Regan himself would shoot 125 rolls of black and white and almost 300 rolls of color during the location.

IN HIS ROLE AS PHOTOGRAPHER, EASTWOOD PRACTICES HIS TECHNIQUE ON SUBJECT STREEP.

FOR CINEMATOGRAPHER JACK GREEN, FILMING PROCEEDED SMOOTHLY. He was not dealing with difficult actors. He liked the book. "My wife gave it to me. She said, 'You'll love it.'" He listened to author Waller's reading of the book on tape in the car and read the script four or five times before going into production. "It's like looking at a classic art piece on the wall. It never seems to get boring," he says. "The biggest challenge was dealing with the thought that millions of copies of that book were sold, that probably each person who read it gave it to another to read, and that all those people have the scenes already in their imaginations. We've got to fulfill or exceed what they visualized—that preconceived, imaginary world of *The Bridges of Madison County*."

When rolling, Green and Bannerman stood next to the camera operator and the boom man. When Eastwood was acting, Bannerman would give the cues to start shooting. During the scene in which Kincaid and Francesca touch for the first time, while dancing to the radio, he almost forgot to say, "Cut." "The dancing scene was exquisite to watch," recalls Bannerman. "When the two interact physically for the first time—it was a wonderful thing to see two actors do." Streep explains that it was Eastwood's sensitivity to the needs of actors that made the scene so romantic. Ordinarily, says Streep, actors have to dance in

ACTOR JIM HAYNIE, WHO PLAYS
RICHARD JOHNSON, POSES WITH HIS
MOVIE WIFE ON THE PORCH OF
HIS SET HOME.

silence; the music is added later. Eastwood had the real music, a Johnny Hartman song, playing as they danced. "It's such a romantic scene, and it really helped that the song was in there," says Streep. The tenderness of the slowly developing relationship affected everyone on the set.

THE SIMPLICITY OF THE PRODUCTION MADE IT EVEN MORE INTIMATE. Green was surprised by the depth of his own response to the shooting. "You get closer, and it gets more intense," he says. "At the end of ten hours, the rest of us had been put through an emotional roller coaster along with the actors. This was probably one of the few times I couldn't finish a day's work without some big emotion."

Streep was frankly astonished. She hadn't seen the Dirty Harry movies. "I doubt he's seen *Ironweed*, either," she says of her succès d'estime with Jack Nicholson. But after seeing *Unforgiven*, she wanted to work with Eastwood the Director. "It was very, very good," she says. "Not wrought—just taking place in front of your eyes. It effortlessly flows." Still, she had reservations about acting opposite someone who was also directing. "They sometimes pull out of the scene and watch," she says. "An actor can feel it. Instead of looking at you, they're watching you."

She waited to see if Eastwood would really lose himself in the role. And, she says, he did. "He was able to be in the scenes with me as Kincaid. When the camera was on him, he did everything that he had to do without a lot of drama. He just opened his heart in this movie, and it's really gorgeous. He was acting, reaching for something further. You find a place within yourself and decide to go there. It's very brave." She smiles in bemusement. "It was thrilling to see him do these emotional scenes. Boom—he was right there. Unashamed. Unafraid. Weeping in front of the crew, then going to stand, still bleary-eyed, behind the camera."

It was cold in the house—there was no heat. Between shots, Streep would wrap up in a robe and knit. If there was a longer break, she retreated to her trailer. By the second week, Streep says, "I was reeling with the pace." She was also

ROLL 'EM: THE CAMERA SHOOTS
EASTWOOD, WHO HIMSELF SHOOTS
ROSEMAN BRIDGE.

wondering how she was doing—Eastwood hadn't said anything to her. Finally, he came up to her and said, she reports, "You know, I don't say much." She laughs, remembering. "That's good," he told her. "That means I like it."

The fast pace, she thought, was good for the actors but tough for the crew. Clearly, however, the crew both expected the pace and reveled in it. "Clint's view is that a happy set is a good-working set. He believes people should have fun," says Green. "And everyone has equal status as a human being. Anytime we have to hump equipment for a long way, Clint makes sure everybody picks up a camera case or a light. He stands in the lunch line like everyone else and waits his turn." Everyone felt at ease. "Because there were no politics—everyone worked together to make the same movie—I found that at the end of the day, I still had some energy left over," says Oppewall.

And the California crew felt quite comfortable with the Iowans. "They treated us as a normal business," says Green. "Sometimes small towns can hate you and treat you like circus people or gypsies. Or they can make a big deal out of you. These people were like, 'Okay, they're here, let's leave 'em alone.'"

TOWNFOLK WHO GOT WORK AS EXTRAS IN THE MOVIE HANG OUT FOR A SCENE IN WINTERSET'S NORTHSIDE CAFE.

MADISON COUNTY, NEVERTHELESS, WAS CURIOUS ABOUT what was going on. The road to the farmhouse was blocked off to all traffic but for school buses and the people who lived nearby. One local kid was fortunate enough to be hired to keep an eye on the weeds by the mailbox reading, Mr. and Mrs. Richard Johnson, lest anyone cut the grasses for souvenirs, thereby ruining the continuity of a shot. But the moviemakers were preparing to emerge in the town of Winterset. "I love shooting films in towns like that, because it's a whole new experience for them," says Bannerman, pointing out that the only other film made in Iowa recently was *Field of Dreams*, shot some three hours away. Oppewall was busy "dressing" the town for its star turn. "I had to do sets for a grocery store, cafe, jazz club, and exterior facades and signs for half of Winterset," she says.

"It was eerie, a time warp," says Sherry Ellis. "Seeing the old cars perfectly placed around the square . . ." The Conoco station that had closed the previous spring became a Texaco station. Fortuitously, one of the biggest collectors of gas station memorabilia lives in West Des Moines, and he had enough props to re-create a '60s Texaco station. The folks of Winterset looked at the gas price on the pumps—34 cents a gallon—and just shook their heads. The video rental store became a furniture store, Midwest Vision got a new sign reading, Midwest Optometrists, Winterset Livestock and Feed became a general store. Darkroom Plus became "For Lease." Said the photo studio's owner, "I just put up my new sign, too."

The Northside Cafe got a new interior—and new waitresses. Tania Mishler, the announcer for the Iowa state lottery, landed a small role serving tables. She had once worked at a restaurant Eastwood owns in Carmel, CA, the Hog's Breath Inn. "It's kind of ironic," she said. "I was a waitress for him there, and now I'm a waitress in the movie. He just smiled when I told him that." Some 500 Madison County hopefuls showed up at the American Legion Hall for the casting call for five speaking parts and 200 extra parts. The North Side Barber

HOLLYWOOD RAINMAKERS GET READY TO
PROVIDE PRECIPITATION IN
FRONT OF A CLASSIC TEXACO STATION.

THE MOVIE'S LEADING MAN FEELS
THE EFFECTS OF THE RAINMAKING
EQUIPMENT ON THE STREETS OF
WINTERSET.

Shop, which fortunately boasted barbers old enough to remember the "zero taper" cut, did the '60s style on some 50 extras. On September 20, shooting began. For her bit part, Shawn Clark, a 16-year-old junior from Winterset High, walked down one side of the street over and over. She got her reward, though: a handshake from the director. "It made my day," she said.

They were really rolling. Every night, script supervisor Kate Haldman went back to the production offices at the West Valley Inn and typed up her notes of what had been shot that day. Some days they shot four to six pages of script rather than the usual one or two. "We never lose time on an Eastwood set," says Bannerman. "And the weather was, in Malpaso's tradition, on our side. When we needed sun, it was sunny. When we needed rain, it rained. We had to cover maybe two times."

One of the exceptions was the critical scene in which Francesca watches Kincaid drive away in the rain. "It didn't rain. Wasn't even overcast," says cinematographer Green. "You would hope that in Iowa with winter approaching, you could get some cloud cover." The Winterset Fire Department rolled out two fire trucks and cranked up the hydrants to feed the moviemakers' sprinkler apparatus, but they couldn't shoot in brilliant sunlight and had to film at dusk. That was the only glitch in the schedule. The summer was almost over.

As the story moved toward its finale, one of the most moving scenes for Streep was the good-bye in the rain, when Francesca sees Kincaid standing there and remains in the truck with her husband. Streep couldn't actually see Eastwood when they shot that final parting. It was only later, when she watched the dailies, that she saw his face. "He looked like a ghost, desolate," she says. "It broke my heart." Eastwood says, "The most emotional scenes are when they realize that she's not going to go with him, that she's going to stay."

That question, endlessly debated by the book's readers, was talked out by the moviemakers as well: why did Francesca stay with children who were soon grown, with a husband who didn't meet her needs? Why did she stay after the children left home, after her husband's death? Why did she stay on, until it was too late and Kincaid was dead? "I think that she just kind of thought that he had another life. She assumed that his life had changed," suggests Eastwood. "She was more in love with the memory of the time they had together." Lagravenese decided that her guilt about leaving husband and children would have soured her relationship with Kincaid: "In order to preserve the love she had with him, she had to give him up. If she had left with him, she would have been just going from one man to another. I wanted her to feel complete at the end."

Meryl Streep's final scene was when an aging Francesca receives a letter from Kincaid's lawyers telling her that he has died and sending her his effects. Prop man Eddie Iona had not followed the usual practice of putting dummy type on the piece of paper. Rather, he had typed up the whole letter from the book on a lawyer's letterhead. Bannerman knew the contents of the letter, and he couldn't believe Streep's virtuosity as he watched her do the scene. "She takes the letter out of the envelope, and you can see the whole letter play on her face as she reads it. She's learning how truthful his love was," he says. "Clint just let the camera roll. No one breathed. Even the crew was tearing up."

THE SUMMER WEATHER WAS OVER, RIGHT ON SCHEDULE. ANNIE Corley, the Broadway actress who plays Francesca's daughter, and Victor Slezak, a stage and TV actor who plays the son, were showing up to shoot their scenes in the dreary autumnal weather. The farmhouse sets had to be modernized to the 1990s for the scenes when the adult kids visited. It took Oppewall's crew two and a half days, with shifts working at night. "We took out small trees, brought in bigger ones. We grew vines into the porch. We aged the exterior, roof and paint, changed some furniture—the stove, refrigerator, put in a microwave, some new slipcovers—and restocked the pantry with new canned goods."

They finished shooting on November 3, ten days ahead of schedule. "He shot me in five weeks," says Streep. "I was home for a month before I got my last paycheck." Says Eastwood proudly, "We shot it in 42 days." The production also came in at a cost of less than $9 million "below the line," or without talent fees, a pittance compared with most movie budgets. "We were able to do that because we had a really great crew and really great cast," says Eastwood. "We didn't have to fiddle a lot, just enough to get everybody comfortable and in the mood."

BETWEEN SHOOTS IN NEW YORK AND LOS ANGELES, PRODUCER KATHLEEN KENNEDY MAKES A FLYING VISIT TO IOWA.

So it was good-bye to Madison County. The redone farmhouse was closed up. The local Winterset paper, *The Madisonian*, endorsed Eastwood for governor of Iowa, calculating that the actor had spent more days in the state than its two senators. The local folks bid the film company adieu with mixed feelings, glad to have life back to normal, but with a feeling of letdown, "like after Christmas," says Ellis. She had put in 93-hour weeks and welcomed 59,000 people to 1994's Covered Bridge Festival. The area, which boasts only two hotels with a total of 47 beds, had become a major destination for romantically minded Japanese honeymooners. Some couples even arranged to get married in the covered bridges, holding services complete with readings from the book. The little book had been on the bestseller list for more than 2 years, and counting. Robert Waller had written three more books, 1994's *Slow Waltz in Cedar Bend*, 1995's *Border Music* and the forthcoming *Puerto Vallarta Squeeze*. He had also left Iowa for a thousand-acre ranch in Alpine, Texas.

IN HER ROLE AS TRANSPLANTED
WAR BRIDE, STREEP MAKES USE OF
EXPRESSIVE ITALIAN HANDS.

IN HIS STUDIO WITH A VIEW OF THE EMPIRE STATE BUILDING, PHOTOGRAPHER Ken Regan takes Polaroids of a pair of assistants to check his lighting. Roy Helland, Meryl Streep's makeup man and hairdresser, turns off the radio and flips on a Maria Callas tape.

Regan gives Meryl Streep a big hug as she arrives. She is walking with a cane since suffering a torn ligament in a fall. She was meant to go to California to pose with Eastwood for the movie poster that will lure audiences into theaters, a romantic shot, but because of her injury, she doesn't want to travel. The two stars are being photographed separately, on opposite coasts; computer magic will later merge the negatives.

"I hate having my picture taken," says this woman who performs before cameras for a living.

"With a passion," concurs Regan. "Clint, too. It's a very strange phenomenon that exists among movie stars. They make their living in motion pictures, but they hate to sit for a still photograph."

Today, Regan is shooting two situations for the poster. One shows the stars in silhouette, gazing at each other with a covered bridge in the background. Regan has already shot the bridge in Iowa, Eastwood in California and now captures Streep's pure profile in New York.

That ordeal over, Streep sits down for a video interview with publicist Marco Barla that will be part of an electronic press kit, material to be sent to television stations to promote the movie. The cameraman wants to do a sound check. "Okay," says Streep. "This is how loud I'll speak unless you get me angry, in which case I'll get real quiet. I learned that from Clint."

She laughs. Helland touches up her hair with a comb.

Barla launches into his interview. "Are the lovers ordinary people?"

"Yes," says Streep. "But together they are extraordinary. Their dreams—those suppressed 'I wish' moments that each had before they met—are realized when they are together.

"The screenplay is not just concerned with four days. It's about the secrets that a life can hold, about how you never really know your parents.

"It was an emotional experience to read, it was an emotional experience to shoot, and when I see the movie in Burbank, that will be an emotional experience, too."

A CONTINENT AWAY, EASTWOOD IS IN THE EDITING ROOM IN PERSON—and on the monitors. "Clint doesn't look at himself as himself, he looks at Robert Kincaid as a character," says Malpaso film editor Joel Cox. "He says, 'If I make a little stumble, don't edit around it. Don't clean it up. It's real.'" The editor won an Academy Award in 1993 for his work on *Unforgiven*. Now Cox is going through footage of *Bridges*, taking the best shots and piecing them together. Iowa being cultivated on a lot in California.

Streep, as Francesca Johnson, stands at the sink.

Cox monitors the sound track on a computer display. He leaps from screen to screen, fast-forwarding until the voices sound like mice. He skips from the tiny windows on his left-hand monitor, each showing a different version of the shot, to the split-screen monitor on the right, playing the computer keyboard like a piano. Until recently, film had to be laboriously cut and pieced together, a long and expensive process. Today, rough footage can be copied onto videotape and easily manipulated using the latest electronic editing software. Only after editing is completed is the actual film stock cut.

The noise of peeling vegetables. Francesca is preparing dinner. Then the sound of a screen door closing, quietly. The sound of water running.

Cox plays the scene over and over, as Eastwood sits quietly, watching. Cox is struggling with the sound of glasses that clink twice rather than once. "I'll open up the track, back up one, and see if that got it," he says. "That should put me back into sync behind it." Cox moves as fast as he can with Eastwood in the room, so as not to waste the boss's time.

"Put it up top," says Eastwood, finally. He usually speaks so softly that one has to strain to hear him, but all of the people who work for him are on alert.

Cox switches the picture to the large monitor above the other two and lets the scene roll all the way through.

"We're almost halfway there," says Eastwood. "I think that scene is fine for the moment. Until we do a complete, finished run-through, we won't touch it."

THE CAMERA CREW SETS UP A FINAL SCENE, IN WHICH FRANCESCA'S CHILDREN THROW HER ASHES OFF OF THE ROSEMAN BRIDGE.

Eastwood declines to predict the success of what should have been a quiet little movie that, along the way, gathered a phenomenal weight of expectation. "I just make it," he says with an echo of his macho screen persona. "If people want to come and see it, fine. If they don't, that's their prerogative." He has other movies in the making.

In a way, making a film is like the relationship between a photographer and a subject, like a serendipitous affair—an intense personal relationship with strangers you may never see again. A separate time, not part of everyday life, yet memorable. Chances are, Streep and Eastwood, like the characters they play, will not see one another again, unless at an official function like an Academy Awards ceremony. "When it's over, you go on to your regular life," says Eastwood. "And the picture has been a great experience—I'll always feel very strongly for Meryl. She's a fabulous talent and a fabulous person." You get the feeling that, unlike some others in Hollywood, Eastwood doesn't use the word *fabulous* often or lightly.

"In the editing room, I'm seeing her every day. She doesn't see me—I see her on film," says Eastwood. "Watching the whole story unfold, I get wonderful memories."

DIRECTOR EASTWOOD FINALLY DISCOVERS WHAT HIS LEADING LADY HAS BEEN KNITTING FOR THE PAST 40 DAYS.

Across town, in front of the Barrymore Building, on the SONY Studio lot, dusk is falling on Kathleen Kennedy's prime parking space, as men in gorilla suits ride back and forth between soundstages on golf carts. Kennedy is working on three pictures, one of which is being directed by Frank Marshall, her husband of eight years, based on *Congo*, Michael Crichton's yarn about a troupe of explorers who stumble on a tribe of mutant, gray gorillas. But there's still a map of Iowa hanging on the wall of Kennedy's office.

Madison County won't forget Hollywood, either. In the end, it took 42 days rather than four, but the affair in the corn fields ended like that of Francesca Johnson and Robert Kincaid, with the departure of the out-of-towners in tears. Gone like the summer, leaving only memories—and some frames of celluloid.

—Claudia Glenn Dowling

Acknowledgments

Thank you:

To Clint for hiring me to do the photography on *The Bridges of Madison County* and for all your support throughout the filming.

To Meryl for being so wonderful and to Roy for his helpful hints in photographing Meryl.

To Joe Hyams for his many years of personal friendship and for helping me build my own bridge with Warner Bros.

To Marco, thanks for sharing your office with me, for being a good friend, and for showing me the Malpaso way.

To Kathleen Kennedy for liking my portfolio. To Anne Marie Stein for promoting my work at Amblin.

Here's to the gang at Warner Bros. for all your help, support, and patience in editing all the film I shot–thanks again Carl Sanrock, Jess Garcia, and Diane Sponsler. To George Nelson, who helped me get started at Warner Bros.; to Vivian Tibbets, for all those screening tickets; and to Bud Rosenthal, for my first cowboy hat from the truck stop in Gallup, *Superman 1*!

To the crew of *Bridges*, and especially Jack Green, Steve Campanelli, Bill Coe, John Waldo, Dean Simmon, Colin Campbell, Dicky Deats, Willie Burton, Marvin Lewis, Eddie Aiona, Cate Hardman, Jeannine Oppewall, Keith Dillin, Michael Maurer, Lisa Becker, and Jason McGatlin.

To the Dell Publishing Alumni Association: Bob Markel, the first editor I worked with out of school. We finally did a book together. Thanks.

Walter Bernard, a great designer and long-time friend–one of the really good guys.

To Milton Glaser, thanks for the great ride. To Chalkley and the staff at WBMG–thanks for everything.

Last but far from least: Suzanne, for your endless work on the film, the book, and every-thing else you have always done for me; thanks also for being such a patient, understand-ing, and loving daughter.

Without whom, etc.:
For Maureen Egen, for making it all happen.
To Michael Harkavy.
To Richard Lagravanese for your last-minute prose.
To Tom and Melissa Rooker–thanks for everything.
To Mom, Lori, and Suzanne–all my love.

–KEN REGAN

Dear Francesca

    I hope this finds
when you'll receive
I'm gone. I'm sixty-fi
been thirteen years si
met when I came up
for directions.

    I'm gambling that
upset your life in
couldn't bear to thin
sitting in a secondha
stove or in some